WHAT CAN I DO?

A Guide To Challenging Your Social Privilege And Taking Action To Change The World

WRITTEN BY
AMANDA R. WILLIAMS

RESEARCHED BY
MCKEL

Table of Contents

INTRODUCTION

Welcome to *What Can I Do?* – an empowering guide to weaving justice work into your life by leveraging your unique social privileges. Congratulations on taking the first step towards responsibility, recognizing that we all play a role in crafting more inclusive, ethical, and just communities for all! While the challenges of injustice loom large, recognizing our ability to take practical steps within our spheres of influence to address it is the foundation of collective progress. With that shared understanding, breaking down pillars of oppression becomes achievable. Undoing social privilege can be realized.

This guide is designed to encourage every one of us to wield our privileges purposefully, shifting oppressive dynamics within the scope of our lives. It is a call to action, rejecting the dominant mode of passivity in the face of seemingly insurmountable forces shaping our world negatively. As human animals, our species membership inherently grants us certain privileges, and many of us have other social privileges on top of that, at varying levels, related to our positionality in society. That means we all have at least a little bit of power to make different choices, to reduce the amount of harm we contribute to the world, and to improve our relationships with the beings who share the world with us.

Some readers may argue that focusing on individual change falls short—that real transformation requires institutional change, which individuals alone cannot achieve. History shows that institutions rarely shift on their own; instead, they tend to uphold the status quo. Recent decades in America remind us that without direct pressure, these structures are unlikely to become more equitable. While this book emphasizes personal responsibility, it acknowledges that individual actions alone are not enough. Lasting change requires both personal and collective efforts: we must change ourselves to generate the pressure needed to reshape institutions toward a more just society.

While the concepts of privilege and justice are universally relevant, this particular guide stays focused on a United States context. The dynamics of privilege can vary significantly depending on the cultural, legal, and historical frameworks of different countries, but in this book, I examine how privilege operates within American systems. The privileges discussed here are shaped by the unique intersections of race, class, gender, and politics in the U.S., where systemic inequalities are often reinforced by longstanding institutional practices. Although the strategies and reflections offered may resonate globally, they are intended primarily for readers navigating the specific social and political landscape of the United States.

This guide serves as more than just a roadmap; it stands as a testament to our individual capacity to mend the social fabric and create meaningful change. While not every privilege category is covered here, eight of the major ones are included. If you identify as a human being, an adult, able-bodied, neurotypical, a cisgender man, heterosexual, white, wealthy, or thin, this guide is relevant to you. If you embody multiple identities mentioned here, your responsibility for taking action is even greater. The entities wielding the most power—governments, courts, corporations, billionaires—are not incentivized to better our world; rather, they sustain the status quo, either designed to foster existing power imbalances or emerged as a result of them. By doing nothing and leaving our privileged statuses unaltered, we also maintain the status quo. We must roll up our sleeves and do the work ourselves to reshape the oppressive power dynamics in society, to demand change by changing ourselves and our own actions. Contributing to societal repair is an ongoing practice and a crucial step toward total liberation. So, when you find yourself thinking, *What can I do to change the world?* pick up this guide and get started.

PART I

SOCIAL PRIVILEGE

WHAT IS PRIVILEGE?

Social privilege is the story of how power relations play out in society. Privilege, defined as "a special, unearned advantage or entitlement benefiting individuals, often unbeknownst to the benefiting groups" (Black & Stone, 2005), has been likened by Michael Kimmel (2018) to "running with the wind at your back." He adds that "it feels like just plain running, and we rarely if ever get a chance to see how we are sustained, supported, and even propelled by that wind."

As an example, imagine two students, one from a financially wealthy family and the other from a low-income household. The student from the affluent family attends a well-funded school with ample resources, smaller class sizes, access to tutors, and a range of extracurricular activities. They have a quiet and comfortable study space at home, and their parents can afford educational materials, books, and even additional educational support if needed. Conversely, the student from the low-income household attends an underfunded school with larger class sizes, limited resources and extracurricular options, and fewer experienced teachers. At home, they might lack a quiet space to study due to crowded living conditions or household responsibilities. Their parents might be working multiple jobs, limiting their ability to provide academic support.

In this scenario, the student from the wealthier background might not fully realize the advantages they have. To them, academic success might feel like 'just plain running' because they're accustomed to these resources and support systems. They might not see how their access to quality education, educational support at home, and a conducive learning environment propels them forward compared to their counterpart facing numerous obstacles due to socioeconomic limitations. This example illustrates how social privilege provides unseen advantages that can significantly impact individuals' opportunities and outcomes, often without them fully realizing the extent of their advantage.

Overall, social privilege can be seen as the inverse to social inequality because its focus is on how power structures in society aid those who are privileged versus how those structures oppress others. It's important to understand the mechanics of privilege in our own lives and society more broadly. Learning about privilege enhances awareness of injustice and fosters both personal and systemic reflection, facilitating positive change. It enables a deeper understanding of how certain groups or individuals possess differing levels of access to societal power and resources. Of course, this topic is intricate as privilege isn't isolated—it intertwines various forms and can manifest differently across diverse situations.

The phrase "Check your privilege" is frequently used across diverse contexts, sparking debates about whether its widespread use has diminished its meaning and impact

(Sebastian, 2020). Some argue that constant references to privilege result in individuals wallowing in guilt rather than actively challenging structural injustice (Malik, 2020). There are even claims that privilege, particularly racial privilege, is non-existent (Rav, 2020). However, scholars studying social privilege generally agree that it is a tangible phenomenon with significant consequences. And when you're someone who lacks certain privileges or does not have full access to them, this disadvantaged experience is very real and shapes the course of your life.

Although privilege is widely acknowledged as a concept, individuals often deny its relevance to their own lives, frequently influenced by socio-economic factors. For example, statements such as "I don't have privilege because I lack financial resources" reflect a common misunderstanding that equates privilege solely with economic status. Gina Crosley-Corcoran (2014) addresses this perspective in an article focusing on white privilege. Despite experiencing severe childhood poverty without basic amenities, she asserts that being born with white skin in America comes with unearned advantages that others do not enjoy. Examples include representation in the media, a white-washed narrative of national heritage and civilization, and avoiding racial profiling by law enforcement, just to name a few. Having privilege does not mean you do not struggle; it means that you are not struggling because you lack that privilege.

It's crucial to recognize that oftentimes privilege operates on a spectrum; not everyone possesses the same degree of a particular privilege. Human-species privilege, inherent to all human animals, exemplifies this concept because not all human animals are treated the same, and some privileges that make up the collection of privileges inside of species privilege may not be accessible to everyone. In a world shaped by white supremacism, for instance, people of color (POC) often face dehumanization and discriminatory treatment, limiting their access to certain aspects of human-species privilege. While the term privilege can be misused and potentially lead to overwhelm, acknowledging it holds power and opens the gates to the possibility of change. Privilege should not be the be-all-end-all of analyses nor the end of a self-improvement checklist. Instead, it is the first step on a long journey toward dismantling oppressive power structures and working to eliminate its existence.

The concept of social privilege is often traced back to the writings of W.E.B. Du Bois, the American sociologist, historian, and civil rights activist, especially in his 1903 book *The Souls of Black Folk*. He wrote about what he called a "double consciousness" that Black people have, a "sense of always looking at one's self through the eyes of others, of measuring one's soul by the tape of a world that looks on in amused contempt and pity" Du Bois observed that while Black people had to know about white Americans and recognize racial discrimination, white people did not think much about Black Americans nor the effects of their discrimination.

In the 1980s, social privilege gained momentum in academia, largely thanks to Peggy McIntosh, an American feminist and anti-racism activist. Her influential 1989 article, "White Privilege and Male Privilege," listed forty-six privileges she experienced as a white person in the U.S., urging readers to scrutinize their own advantages in complex power dynamics. In her 1989 piece, "White Privilege: Unpacking the Invisible Knapsack," McIntosh underscores the interconnectedness of societal hierarchies, shedding light on white privilege often disregarded. McIntosh's early work catalyzed heightened scholarly interest in privilege.

Privilege, once largely confined to theoretical and academic discussions, now permeates mainstream social justice conversations—for instance, in popular discourse around topics like workplace diversity, accessibility, and racial bias—shedding light on everyday power dynamics. Essentially, privilege embodies a form of social and cultural power. However, the manifestation of privilege is intricate due to our multifaceted identities, diverse socioeconomic backgrounds, and varied access to privilege. In her essay "In the Doing and the Being," Lori B. Girshick (2014) points out, "Any existing oppression tends to support the others because the framework of privilege operates through them all" (pp. 54-62). This framework provides a lens to discern the advantages certain individuals possess and the disadvantages others face, offering insights into group power dynamics and interconnections among different forms of oppression.

Understanding privilege requires an appreciation of its inherent complexity and intersectional nature. Kimberlé Crenshaw (1989) introduced the concept of intersectionality to explore how various forms of privilege and oppression interconnect, describing it as a "way of thinking about identity and its relationship to power." For instance, someone might hold privileges A, B, and C but lack privileges D, E, and F, creating a unique interplay within their lived experience. This variation highlights how different privileges intersect in diverse ways; privilege A might interact distinctly with privilege F compared to E.

Intersectionality, as described by Crenshaw, clarifies how social identities—such as race, gender, sexuality, class, and even species (although Crenshaw fails to include this category)—shape systems of advantage and disadvantage. Melanie Joy (2019), in *Powerarchy*, underscores this complexity, noting that humans inherently possess "species privilege" in power hierarchies, or powerarchies, where animals are typically placed at a disadvantage. She explains, "All of us navigate multiple realities, assuming diverse roles within a given system. We each carry certain forms of privilege while also belonging to oppressed groups." In this sense, someone belonging to multiple oppressed groups still retains privilege simply by virtue of being human.

Indigenous scholar Margaret Robinson (2017), in her conversations with Julia Feliz Brueck in *Veganism in an Oppressive World*, also emphasizes the value of intersectionality in understanding how racialization, ability, gender, and other categories of identity intersect to shape experiences of advantage and marginalization. For example, experiences of privilege vary considerably: being white and queer involves different social dynamics compared to being Black and queer, disabled and queer, or adding other factors like socio-economic status.

Additionally, individuals may hold varying degrees of privilege even within the same category (Croteau, Talbot, Lance, & Evans, 2002). This interconnected nature of privilege and oppression reveals that each identity—whether based on race, gender, or species—affects one's experiences of privilege and discrimination within broader systems of power.

Other scholars suggest that intersectionality may be too limiting in a discussion of species privilege specifically. David Pellow (2014), for example, in his book *Total Liberation*, argues that because intersectionality "begins and ends with humans," it is "unnecessarily restrictive." He says, "one cannot fully grasp the foundations of racism, classism, ableism, heterosexism, and patriarchy without also understanding speciesism and dominionism because they are all ideologies and practices rooted in hierarchy and the creation of oppositional superior and inferior subjects". The hierarchy is a relationship dynamic that consistently creates power imbalances among different groups and individuals, resulting in the emergence of privilege. Changing relationships of hierarchy features heavily in the antidote to social privilege.

Most large categories of privilege are made up of a collection of individual privileges. Gender privilege, for instance, contains within it privileges such as men getting paid more than women and men having more reproductive autonomy than women. Species privilege, too, is a category of privilege made up of an assorted list of singular privileges, from the cultural assumption that human animals have the right to dominate and use other animals for their own benefit to having the freedom to go wherever you want when you want. Everyone has their own list of privileges based on the unique circumstances of everyone's life. In an effort to understand others, pattrice jones, in her book *The Oxen at the Intersection*, reminds us to consider social circumstances, saying that "Everything humans do to animals or their habitats is done by humans in particular social, economic, and environmental circumstances—all of which have been shaped by sexism, racism, and other forms of oppression among human beings."

If we were to create a list of our privileges, as McIntosh created a list of her own privileges in 1989, it would be from the perspective of our own life experience and would not apply entirely to all other human animals. Even so, list commonalities can still be observed among similarly circumstanced individuals. Such is the case for human-species privilege, which in one way or other advantages the human animal over other living beings with whom we share the planet. All of that said, one of the main reasons to understand one's own privileges is to use the platform that those privileges grant to challenge the systems that produce these advantaged and disadvantaged realities. It is up to all of us to actively work towards reshaping power dynamics and reducing our own undeserved privileges whenever we can.

A NOTE ABOUT SELF CARE

Before throwing ourselves into the work of social transformation, we must prioritize our own self-care. To truly give back to the world and others, we must first ensure our own needs are met. Much like how a tree needs strong roots to bear fruit, we too need a solid foundation of self-care to thrive and give generously. When we prioritize our mental, emotional, and physical well-being, we are better equipped to show up in the world with authenticity, energy, and a deep sense of purpose. Without caring for ourselves first, we risk burnout, exhaustion, and losing sight of who we are, which can diminish the quality and sincerity of what we have to offer.

By tending to our own well-being, we are not being selfish—rather, we are creating a foundation for sustainable giving. Research in positive psychology suggests that self-care practices enhance our emotional resilience and improve our capacity for empathy and social connectedness (Neff, 2003; Fredrickson, 2001). In nurturing ourselves, we unlock the ability to genuinely connect with others and contribute meaningfully. Without this self-care, our efforts may become strained or depleted, limiting our ability to fully support the causes and people we care about. Meeting our personal needs creates the space to give with compassion, allowing us to engage in ways that are both impactful and enduring. Once our needs are met, we are better positioned to actively work toward reducing our social privilege, as the motivation to contribute to social equity often stems from a secure foundation of personal well-being (Brown, 2012; Maslow, 1943).

A NOTE ABOUT RELIGION

While this guide addresses several key forms of social privilege, it does not specifically cover religious privilege, a form with significant impact in the United States. Christian privilege, as described by scholars such as Khyati Joshi (2006), pervades various aspects of public life, from social norms to governmental structures, positioning Christianity as the assumed cultural default. This dominance often marginalizes individuals of other faiths or those without religious affiliation. Joshi's research highlights how policies, cultural norms, and public celebrations frequently align with Christian practices and holidays, subtly reinforcing this privilege and shaping the experiences of non-Christians in both personal and public spheres.

However, I've chosen not to explore religious privilege in depth in this guide for a few reasons. First, as someone who is not religious and views organized religion critically, I find it challenging to approach the topic with the fairness and nuance it deserves. Religion is deeply complex and personal for many people. Second, this guide is intended to be a concise, actionable resource, and religious privilege—particularly in the ways it intersects with race, class, gender, and other identities—would require a much more extensive discussion. By focusing on other categories of privilege, I aim to offer clear, effective guidance. For readers interested in understanding religious privilege further, I recommend Khyati Y. Joshi's *Christian Privilege: Breaking a Sacred Taboo*, which provides an in-depth analysis of how Christian privilege shapes U.S. society, especially in education and government.

HOW TO REDUCE YOUR PRIVILEGE

Social privilege manifests in various forms, offering unearned advantages to individuals based on race, gender, class, species, and other social categories. The journey to eliminate social privilege is challenging but necessary for creating a more equitable society. This guide outlines a three-step approach—Education, Self-Reflection, and Action—to help individuals and communities reduce social privilege effectively. Below you will find the three steps explained as well as two examples of how to use these steps in the real world.

Step 1: Education

Education plays a crucial role in understanding social privilege and its impact. By actively seeking out diverse perspectives, reading literature on social justice issues, attending workshops or seminars, and engaging with marginalized communities, individuals can broaden their understanding of privilege and its implications. Education helps dismantle ignorance and fosters empathy, which are essential steps towards combating systemic inequalities.

Step 2: Self Reflection

Self-reflection is another powerful tool in addressing social privilege. Taking the time to critically examine one's beliefs, biases, and behaviors allows individuals to identify areas where privilege may be influencing their thoughts and actions. Engaging in introspection helps uncover unconscious biases and promotes personal growth. By reflecting on how privilege operates in their own lives, individuals can become more mindful of their interactions and work towards being better allies to marginalized groups.

Step 3: Action

Participation in action is key to translating knowledge and self-awareness into tangible change. This can involve supporting social justice initiatives, challenging discriminatory practices, advocating for policy reform, or participating in community activism. By actively standing up against injustice, individuals can use their privilege to amplify the voices of marginalized individuals and contribute to creating a more equitable society. Taking action not only benefits those facing oppression but also allows individuals to align their actions with their values.

Let's imagine Alex, someone aiming to better understand and address social privilege in their daily life. Coming from a background with considerable economic (they are financially wealthy) and racial (they are white) privilege, Alex follows three key steps: Education, Self-Reflection, and Action.

Step 1: Education

Alex starts by acknowledging that their background—having benefited from privileges related to race, economic stability, and access to quality education—might create blind spots in understanding others' experiences. Recognizing this, Alex takes a proactive role in educating themselves. They read foundational works such as *The New Jim Crow* by Michelle Alexander and *So You Want to Talk About Race* by Ijeoma Oluo to explore how systemic racism and privilege function in society. Alex also attends social justice workshops at a community center, participates in webinars on allyship, and seeks out personal narratives from marginalized groups through podcasts, social media, and local community events. Through this, Alex begins to see how privilege has shaped their worldview, sometimes at the expense of understanding others' struggles.

Step 2: Self-Reflection

With a stronger educational foundation, Alex moves to self-reflection. They start journaling to examine how privileges—such as racial and economic privileges—have influenced their life. For instance, Alex realizes that attending a well-funded school afforded them educational opportunities not accessible to many, often due to systemic inequalities. They reflect on past assumptions, uncovering unconscious biases about others' socioeconomic status or racial backgrounds. This self-reflection helps Alex confront areas where privilege has shielded them from facing challenges others routinely encounter, such as discrimination in education or employment.

Step 3: Action

Now equipped with knowledge and a deeper understanding of

their privilege, Alex is ready to act. They begin by supporting local social justice initiatives, like volunteering with an organization advocating for housing equity, a crucial issue they previously felt distanced from. In the workplace, Alex leverages their privilege to champion inclusive policies, pushing for diverse hiring practices and mentorship programs for underrepresented groups. They also use their influence to amplify the voices of marginalized colleagues, ensuring that others' contributions are acknowledged in meetings and initiatives. In their personal life, Alex regularly donates to organizations fighting inequality and participates in local rallies advocating for policy reforms to combat systemic racism and economic inequity.

In this scenario, Alex's journey through education, self-reflection, and action demonstrates how acknowledging and addressing privileges can lead to impactful personal growth and meaningful contributions toward social justice. By aligning their actions with their values, Alex helps foster a more equitable environment for others and consciously leverages their privilege to support systemic change.

Now, let's imagine Alex becoming aware of their privilege as a human animal and deciding to take steps to address this in the context of human species privilege and animal rights. Here's how they could apply the same three steps of Education, Self-Reflection, and Action:

Step 1: Education

Alex starts to realize that, as a human, they benefit from species privilege—humans are often placed above other animals, which can lead to the exploitation and suffering of other animals. To educate themselves, Alex reads books like *Animal Oppression and Human Violence* by David Nibert and *Beasts of Burden: Animal and Disability Liberation* by Sunaura Taylor. They watch documentaries like *Dominion* and *Cowspiracy* that expose the impact of human activities on other animals and the environment. Alex also attends seminars on animal ethics and engages in discussions with activists who advocate for Earth and animal liberation. Through this process, Alex begins to understand how industries such as animal agriculture, animal testing, and habitat destruction perpetuate harm to animals and the Earth for the sole benefit of humans.

Step 2: Self-Reflection

With this new knowledge, Alex takes time to reflect on how their daily choices contribute to the exploitation of animals. They realize that their diet, purchasing habits, and entertainment choices (like visiting zoos or circuses) have supported industries that harm animals. Alex becomes aware of how easy it is for humans to ignore the lives and wellbeing of other animals because of their species privilege. They start journaling about these realizations, considering the ethical implications of their choices and recognizing where they've been indifferent to the suffering of other species. This reflection helps Alex see that they've unconsciously accepted norms that prioritize human convenience over animal welfare.

Step 3: Action

Determined to align their actions with their newfound awareness, Alex takes several steps to reduce their participation in systems that harm animals. First, they transition to a plant-based diet to reduce their contribution to animal suffering and environmental destruction. They also begin purchasing cruelty-free products that aren't tested on animals and avoid entertainment venues that exploit animals for profit, such as farms, circuses, or marine parks. Alex starts advocating for animal rights by joining a local group that organizes protests against animal cruelty and raises awareness about veganism. Additionally, Alex uses their social media platforms to amplify the voices of animal rights activists and share educational resources on the impacts of species privilege. They donate to organizations working to end the exploitation of other species and even get involved in campaigns advocating for stronger animal and environmental protection laws.

Through these actions, Alex works to dismantle their human species privilege, choosing to live in a way that honors the lives of all beings—human and more-than-human. Their journey helps to promote compassion for animals and inspires others to rethink their relationship with other species. Alex's alignment of their values with their actions creates positive change for animals and contributes to a broader movement towards animal and Earth justice.

PART II

SPECIFIC PRIVILEGES

I AM AN ADULT

Childhood is the first oppression. Adults enjoy privileges that are systematically denied to children, reinforcing a profound societal inequity. Alfie Kohn (2005), in *Unconditional Parenting*, argues that children are often treated not as individuals with their own rights and autonomy, but as objects to be controlled and shaped by adult authority. From an early age, children are expected to conform to norms dictated by adults, often through coercion and discipline, which reflects a power dynamic based on adult supremacy. This relationship, rooted in the expectation that children must obey and adults must dominate, conditions children to view oppressive structures as natural, setting the stage for societal hierarchies that perpetuate throughout their lives.

One of the first lessons children learn is how to navigate these oppressive dynamics. In *Unconditional Parenting*, Kohn discusses how traditional parenting methods focus on compliance and control rather than fostering independent thought and mutual respect. Schools, which often mirror capitalist ideals, further instill this dynamic by prioritizing obedience and productivity over critical thinking or emotional development. Children are conditioned to see authority figures as inherently superior, a view that later translates into their adult relationships, workplaces, and broader societal structures. Scholar bell hooks (2000) also emphasizes how family units often replicate this hierarchical dynamic, where children are socialized into passive roles of subordination. This system not only oppresses children but also primes them to accept and perpetuate oppression in their adult lives.

Moreover, the authoritarian nature of adult-child relationships teaches children to oppress others. As they grow up, many adopt the same hierarchical mindset that was imposed on them, assuming positions of dominance over others when given the opportunity. This learned behavior sustains the very structures of oppression they grew up with, making it harder to dismantle systems of inequality. Philippe Ariès (1962), in his landmark work *Centuries of Childhood*, explores how modern Western society has historically treated children as extensions of adult will rather than autonomous individuals, showing that the roots of this oppression run deep into cultural and historical contexts. The failure to challenge this dynamic in childhood reverberates throughout society, influencing how we interact with others and perpetuate power imbalances.

To counteract this cycle of oppression, it is crucial that adults treat children as equally valuable fellow humans with their own unique minds, bodies, and points of view. This requires respecting children's autonomy, including their bodily autonomy, by not forcing physical affection and by standing up for their rights and safety. Protecting vulnerable populations of children, such as transgender kids—those whose gender identity differs from the sex they were assigned at birth—is particularly urgent in a society where laws are being proposed and enacted that jeopardize their safety. Adults must actively fight for policies that defend the rights of children and resist those that seek to control and endanger them. Sociologist Viviana Zelizer (1985), in *Pricing the Priceless Child*, underscores the ways in which children's rights have historically been overlooked in favor of their economic utility or sentimental value, further illustrating the systemic disregard for children's autonomy.

By fostering environments where children are treated with genuine respect and dignity, we can begin to dismantle the societal structures that perpetuate oppression. This transformation starts with everyday actions—recognizing children as autonomous individuals, validating their unique perspectives, and consistently advocating for their rights. In doing so, we cultivate a society where both children and adults can flourish, nurtured in an atmosphere of mutual respect. This approach not only preserves their dignity but also breaks the cycle of oppressive relationships that pervade our world, creating space for a more compassionate and equitable future.

Actions Adults Can Take

---

1. Honor Children's Autonomy
- Allow children to make age-appropriate decisions for themselves, respecting their choices and preferences without imposing adult authority unnecessarily.

2. Validate Children's Feelings and Experiences
- Acknowledge and affirm the emotions and perspectives of children, ensuring they feel heard and understood.

3. Respect Bodily Autonomy
- Avoid forcing physical affection, such as hugs or kisses, and teach children that they have control over their own bodies.

4. Communicate with Respect
- Speak to children in the same respectful tone you would use with adults, avoiding condescension, manipulation, or dismissiveness.

5. Engage in Collaborative Problem-Solving
- Involve children in discussions and decisions that affect them, encouraging shared solutions rather than enforcing top-down decisions.

6. Be an Authority in Their Lives, Not Over Them
- Guide and support children by offering wisdom, boundaries, and care, rather than wielding power or control over them. Focus on being a resource they can trust, rather than a figure to fear.

7. Model Empathy and Non-Authoritarian Behavior
- Show understanding and compassion when interacting

with children, demonstrating conflict resolution through dialogue rather than dominance.

8. Challenge Traditional Hierarchies
- Actively question and push back against societal norms that reinforce adult superiority or infantilize children.

9. Support Children's Rights Organizations
- Actively engage with and support groups that advocate for children's rights and well-being, whether through donations, volunteer work, or policy advocacy.

10. Support Children's Rights
- Advocate for policies and laws that protect children's well-being, autonomy, and safety, including the rights of the most marginalized children, such as LGBTQ+ youth, youth of color, and economically disadvantaged youth.

11. Educate Yourself on Child Development
- Learn about child psychology and development to better understand their capacities and needs, reducing the likelihood of unfair expectations.

12. Create Safe Spaces for Expression
- Offer children spaces where they feel safe to voice their thoughts and emotions without fear of punishment or judgment.

13. Empower Self-Advocacy
- Teach children to advocate for themselves by encouraging them to express their needs, set boundaries, and seek help when necessary.

14. Avoid Punishment-Based Discipline
- Shift from punitive approaches to those that focus on

teaching, empathy, and understanding, emphasizing the child's learning and growth.

32

I AM
A HUMAN

Human species privilege refers to the individual, societal, and systemic advantages that human animals hold over other species. It's one of the most under-acknowledged and under-discussed social privileges (Nibert, 2002). It manifests in the ways humans exploit other animals, control ecosystems, and dominate the planet's resources, often without recognizing the intrinsic value of more-than-human life—living beings and ecological entities beyond the human species, including animals, plants, and entire ecosystems. Much like other forms of privilege—such as those based on race, gender, or economic status—species privilege operates largely unnoticed by those who benefit from it, as it is ingrained in cultural norms, legal systems, and economic structures. This concept challenges anthropocentric views that place humans at the top of a hierarchical ladder, suggesting instead that this privilege fosters exploitation and environmental degradation.

Historically, the dominance of human beings over other species has been justified through religious, philosophical, and scientific ideologies that depict humans as superior. In the Western tradition, thinkers like Aristotle viewed animals as existing solely for human use, a belief that influenced later justifications for the mass exploitation of animals through industrial farming, experimentation, and habitat destruction (Singer, 1975). Similarly, Judeo-Christian doctrines often assert that humans are meant to "subdue" the earth and its creatures, reinforcing speciesist attitudes that place human interests above those of other living beings (White, 1967). These deep-seated ideologies have permeated legal frameworks, where animals are classified as property rather than sentient beings with rights, further entrenching species privilege.

The environmental consequences of human species privilege are profound. As humans continue to expand industrial and agricultural activities, they disrupt ecosystems and contribute to the extinction of countless species. The anthropocentric worldview that privileges human life over other forms has led to practices such as deforestation, climate change, and ocean acidification, all of which disproportionately affect more-than-humans (Crist, 2012). These environmental impacts raise ethical concerns about the long-term viability of the planet and challenge the moral justification for placing human needs above those of other species.

Moreover, human species privilege is not just about the exploitation of animals but also about the marginalization of the rights of nature itself. The concept of "earth rights" or recognizing ecosystems as having legal standing has gained traction in recent years, with legal frameworks in countries like Ecuador and New Zealand beginning to challenge anthropocentric models (Kauffman & Martin, 2017). These movements argue that just as human societies are beginning to recognize the harms of racial and gender privilege, it is also necessary to confront the harm caused by human dominance over other species and ecosystems.

In conclusion, human species privilege is a systemic issue deeply rooted in cultural, religious, and legal systems that prioritize human interests over those of other species. Its consequences are far-reaching, leading not only to the exploitation of animals but also to environmental degradation and the marginalization of ecological rights. As global environmental challenges intensify, addressing human species privilege is critical to fostering a more sustainable and ethically responsible relationship between humans and the natural world.

Actions Humans Can Take

1. Adopt a Plant-Based Diet
- Eliminating the consumption of animal products—when their use is unnecessary, meaning not required for survival or health—can help decrease one's contribution to animal suffering and the demand for industrial animal farming, which is harmful to animals and the environment.

2. Support Animal Rights Legislation
- Advocate for laws and policies that protect animals from exploitation, cruelty, and habitat destruction. Support legal frameworks that recognize animals as living beings rather than property.

3. Reduce Consumption of Animal Products Beyond Food
- Avoid purchasing products made from animals, such as leather, fur, and cosmetics tested on animals, to minimize the exploitation of other species where you can.

4. Protect and Restore Natural Habitats
- Participate in or support efforts to conserve wildlife habitats and protect ecosystems from further destruction. This can include volunteering for conservation projects or donating to environmental organizations.

5. Advocate for Legal Recognition of Nature's Rights
- Support movements that seek to give legal rights to ecosystems, rivers, forests, and other natural entities, recognizing their intrinsic value beyond their utility to humans.

6. Reduce Carbon Footprint
- Lower your personal contribution to climate change, which disproportionately affects other species, by

adopting sustainable practices such as using renewable energy, reducing waste, and minimizing travel.

7. Engage in Wildlife and Ecosystem Advocacy

- Speak out against deforestation, pollution, and industrial activities that harm wildlife. Support organizations working to halt activities like logging, mining, and fishing.

8. Practice Sustainable Consumption

- Reduce, reuse, repair, and recycle to minimize the environmental impact of your lifestyle, recognizing that excessive consumption contributes to habitat destruction and resource depletion.

9. Educate Others About Speciesism

- Raise awareness about human species privilege and speciesism by discussing these issues with friends, family, and your community. Encourage others to adopt more ethical attitudes toward other animals and the environment.

10. Reduce Use of Harmful Chemicals

- Limit or eliminate the use of harmful chemicals, such as pesticides and herbicides, which destroy ecosystems and harm wildlife, opting for natural and sustainable alternatives.

11. Participate in Citizen Science Projects

- Get involved in citizen science initiatives that monitor wildlife, document biodiversity, or track environmental changes. This helps provide data to protect species and ecosystems.

12. Do Not Support Zoos and Circuses

- Avoid supporting businesses that exploit animals for

entertainment, such as traditional zoos and circuses, and instead support sanctuaries and ethical rehabilitation centers.

13. Be Mindful of Language

- Avoid using "it" when referring to other species, as this language inherently objectifies them and diminishes their value compared to humans, who are typically referred to with personhood pronouns. Instead, consider using gender-neutral pronouns like "they/them" for all beings, human and more-than-human alike, to reinforce the idea that all species have intrinsic worth and individuality.

14. Advocate for Climate Action

- Support policies and initiatives aimed at combating climate change, as global warming significantly affects all living beings on Earth.

15. Create Wildlife Corridors in Urban and Suburban Areas

- Promote or participate in projects that build safe pathways or "corridors" for wildlife to move freely through urban and suburban environments. This can involve modifying fencing, planting native vegetation, and installing wildlife crossings to reduce roadkill and help animals access essential resources.

16. Promote Coexistence with Local Wildlife

- Encourage a shift from elimination or removal of animals considered "pests" toward coexistence strategies. Use humane, non-lethal methods to address issues with local wildlife, advocate for awareness in your community, and create wildlife-friendly spaces, such as pollinator gardens, to support biodiversity.

17. Learn About and Support Nonviolent Advocacy Against Animal Exploitation

- Explore and consider supporting groups that work to raise awareness about animal exploitation through nonviolent advocacy. This can include initiatives such as rescues, undercover investigations, or organized gatherings at locations where animals are impacted (e.g., factory farms, fur farms, zoos, laboratories). These efforts aim to expose industry practices, advocate for animal welfare, and engage the public in conversations about ethical alternatives.

18. Learn About Civil Disobedience for Ecosystem Protection

- Consider studying civil disobedience movements dedicated to safeguarding critical habitats. In these movements, individuals may engage in actions—such as sit-ins, public demonstrations, or symbolic acts like temporarily blocking machinery or positioning themselves near vulnerable ecosystems—to raise awareness about threats from activities like logging, mining, or oil drilling. Although sometimes controversial due to their potential to disrupt business operations, delay projects, or challenge legal boundaries, these actions aim to highlight the importance of prioritizing ecosystem health and species preservation over economic gain.

I AM
ABLE-BODIED
OR
NEUROTYPICAL

Ability and neurotypical privilege refer to the unearned societal advantages that people who are able-bodied or neurotypical (those whose brain functions and cognitive abilities align with societal norms) experience over individuals with disabilities or neurodivergence. This privilege manifests in the physical and social structures that are designed for those who fit normative ideas of physical and mental function, often leaving disabled or neurodivergent people to face significant barriers. These barriers extend beyond mere inconvenience, affecting access to public spaces, opportunities for employment, healthcare, social interaction, and overall quality of life (Friedman & Owen, 2017). As society continues to push for greater equity in many realms, it is essential to examine the privileges that those with able-bodied and neurotypical identities may overlook in daily life, and to take steps to make spaces and systems more inclusive for all.

One critical perspective in challenging ability and neurotypical privilege is recognizing that disability is not a deviation from the norm but rather a natural and intrinsic part of human diversity. Just as people vary in their race, gender, and sexual orientation, so too do they vary in physical and cognitive abilities. Disability, whether visible or invisible, is a part of the spectrum of human experience and should be viewed as such. Disability studies scholars argue that our society's tendency to treat able-bodiedness as the default and disability as a flaw reflects deeply entrenched biases rather than an understanding of the human condition's complexity (Goodley, 2014). Embracing this diversity means not only accommodating people with disabilities but also valuing their unique perspectives and contributions.

Advocacy plays a crucial role in addressing ableism and neurotypical privilege. One of the key elements of creating an inclusive society is ensuring that spaces are not only compliant with the Americans with Disabilities Act (ADA), but also truly welcoming and accessible. This includes advocating for larger spaces to accommodate wheelchairs, the inclusion of interpreters for Deaf or blind individuals at events, and the installation of ramps and elevators to support those with mobility issues (Stein, 2021). While ADA compliance is a legal minimum, true inclusivity goes beyond laws—it requires a proactive approach to accessibility that centers the lived experiences of disabled individuals.

Understanding the lived experiences of neurodivergent and disabled individuals is essential, as society is often 'not user-friendly' for those who navigate the world differently. Disabilities and neurodivergence can require significant physical and mental energy. Between frequent medical appointments and the challenges of functioning in spaces designed with able-bodied and neurotypical people in mind, many disabled or neurodivergent individuals may have less energy for work, school, or social activities. This may lead to rescheduled plans or additional sick days, which can be misinterpreted by others. As disability advocate Alice Wong (2020) notes, 'The world is largely built by and for non-disabled people, creating daily barriers and demands that deplete energy and limit full participation.' It is vital to approach these situations with empathy, patience, and a belief in the experiences they share. Dismissing or doubting the challenges faced by people with disabilities or neurodivergence only reinforces their isolation and perpetuates ableism (Dunn, 2019). Moreover, communication plays a pivotal role in fostering inclusive interactions. One harmful aspect of able-bodied privilege is the tendency to infantilize or dismiss people with disabilities by addressing their companions or aides rather than speaking to them directly. Talking down to someone with a disability assumes they are less capable or intelligent, a form of microaggression that reinforces societal hierarchies (Mingus, 2011). A simple, yet powerful action is to engage disabled or neurodivergent individuals with the same level of respect and directness afforded to able-bodied and neurotypical people. This can have a profound impact on how included and respected they feel in various spaces.

Social and physical isolation is another challenge often faced by those with disabilities or neurodivergence. Participating in group activities or even navigating public spaces can be overwhelming or inaccessible for some. To address this, people who hold able-bodied and neurotypical privileges can take steps to ensure that their friends, family, and colleagues are included, whether that means sitting with them in less crowded areas, opting for smaller social gatherings, or simply reaching out to make them feel remembered. Social inclusion goes beyond just physical presence—it is about creating environments where everyone feels comfortable, welcome, and valued, regardless of ability (Goodley, 2014).

Another important area where privilege manifests is the workplace. Employers who recognize the diversity of needs in their workforce can play a key role in dismantling ableism. Allowing employees, particularly those with disabilities or neurodivergence, the flexibility to work in ways that suit their needs can make a significant difference in their productivity and well-being. For instance, offering virtual meeting options, making spaces accessible, providing captions or interpreters, and being open to various communication preferences are practical steps toward inclusivity. Research shows that workplaces that adopt flexible and supportive policies see improvements in employee satisfaction and performance, benefiting everyone involved (Petriglieri et al., 2019).

Addressing sensory sensitivities, such as being mindful of scents or adjusting lighting, is another often-overlooked way to be inclusive. Neurodivergent individuals, particularly those with conditions such as autism or sensory processing disorders, may have heightened sensitivity to stimuli that neurotypical individuals can easily overlook. By creating environments where people can feel comfortable—whether at work, social events, or in public spaces—society moves one step closer to equitable inclusivity for all.

Overall, addressing ability and neurotypical privilege requires ongoing awareness, open communication, and a willingness to adapt. Everyone's experience with their body, mind, or disability is unique. Rather than making assumptions, it is vital to ask people what they need and how they prefer to navigate the world. Creating inclusive spaces, both physically and socially, is not only a moral imperative but also enriches communities by ensuring that everyone can participate fully and comfortably. By recognizing and addressing the privileges that able-bodied and neurotypical individuals enjoy, we can work toward a society where all people, regardless of ability, are treated with the dignity, respect, and equity they deserve.

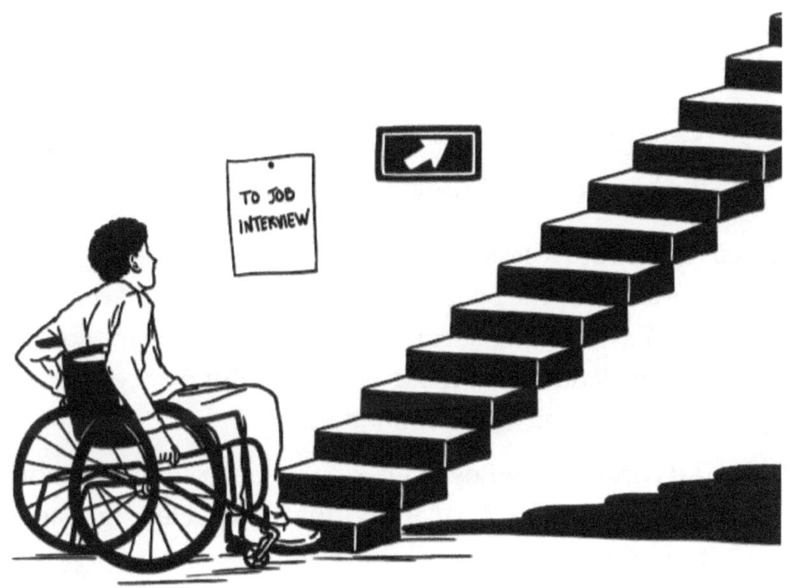

Actions Able-Bodied and/or Neurotypical Folks Can Take

1. Educate Yourself

- Learn about the experiences of people with disabilities and neurodivergence. Read books, watch documentaries, and follow advocates who focus on disability rights and neurodiversity.

- Familiarize yourself with the Americans with Disabilities Act (ADA) and other relevant legislation to understand the basic rights of disabled individuals.

2. Advocate for Accessible Spaces

- Ensure that the spaces you frequent (workplaces, social spaces, public venues) are not only ADA-compliant but also welcoming to those with mobility devices, sensory needs, and other accommodations.

- Advocate for wheelchair ramps, accessible restrooms, interpreters for Deaf individuals, and clear signage in public spaces.

- Encourage event organizers to provide accommodations such as captions, interpreters, or quiet spaces at public and social gatherings.

3. Use Inclusive Language

- Avoid using ableist language and slurs. Phrases like "crazy," "lame," or "dumb" reinforce harmful stereotypes.

- Use gender-neutral pronouns like "they/them" when referring to people whose preferences you do not know and avoid using "it" to refer to individuals, whether human or more-than-human.

4. Respect Energy Levels and Needs

- Be patient and understanding with friends or colleagues who may need to cancel plans or take breaks due to fatigue or overstimulation.

- Check in with friends, colleagues, or family members who may need accommodation to participate in activities. Ask them what they need to feel comfortable.

- Offer flexible scheduling in social or work settings, allowing for rest breaks, remote options, and reduced workloads when necessary.

5. Challenge Ableism in Your Workplace

- Advocate for flexible work arrangements that allow employees to work in ways that suit their physical and mental needs, including remote work, flexible hours, or personalized accommodations.

- Ensure that all meetings have options like virtual attendance, captions, interpreters, and clear communication about what will be expected.

- Encourage your employer to offer accommodations proactively rather than waiting for someone to request them.

6. Foster Inclusive Social Circles

- Invite disabled or neurodivergent friends to social gatherings and ensure those events are accessible and accommodating to their needs.

- Offer to sit with friends in quieter areas during events or stay home with them if they feel overstimulated or uncomfortable in crowded spaces.

- Be mindful of sensory sensitivities by reducing strong

scents, adjusting lighting, and avoiding overwhelming environments when possible.

7. Communicate Clearly

- Make sure your communication is clear and concise, especially when plans change. For some neurodivergent individuals, last-minute changes or unclear instructions can be stressful.

- Use accessible communication methods, such as large-print documents, captions for videos, and providing information in multiple formats (visual, written, spoken).

8. Support Disabled and Neurodivergent Individuals Online

- Share content from disability rights and neurodivergent advocates on social media to raise awareness.

- Call out ableism and neurotypical privilege when you see it, both online and in real life. Use your platform to amplify marginalized voices.

9. Encourage Inclusive Play and Learning for Children

- Foster inclusive play environments for children by encouraging playdates with neurodivergent or disabled kids. Talk to the parents to ensure activities are accessible.

- Teach children about disability and neurodiversity as part of normal human diversity, promoting acceptance and understanding from an early age.

10. Be Mindful of Sensory Sensitivities

- Be aware of how your own habits, such as wearing perfumes, playing loud music, or using bright lights, might affect neurodivergent individuals who are sensitive to sensory input.

- When organizing events, ask attendees if they have

sensory sensitivities and adjust accordingly by offering quiet spaces or dimming lights.

11. Advocate for Policy Changes

- Support legislation and policies that promote accessibility and inclusivity in public spaces, transportation, education, and healthcare.

- Participate in local and national advocacy efforts aimed at improving accessibility, healthcare rights, and disability protections.

12. Challenge Stereotypes and Misconceptions

- When you hear people make assumptions about a disabled or neurodivergent person's capabilities, challenge those stereotypes.

- Avoid speaking for disabled individuals or neurodivergent people—allow them to voice their own needs and experiences.

13. Volunteer with or Donate to Disability Advocacy Organizations

- Support organizations that advocate for disability rights, neurodivergence awareness, and accessibility improvements.

I AM A CISGENDER MAN

Male privilege refers to the societal advantages that men, particularly cisgender men—those whose gender identity aligns with the sex they were assigned at birth—experience simply because of their gender. These advantages manifest in various aspects of life, from professional and social environments to everyday interactions. Male privilege is often invisible to those who benefit from it, making it difficult for many men to recognize and address. This privilege operates within patriarchal systems that grant men certain freedoms and opportunities while limiting or dismissing the experiences and contributions of women, trans individuals (whose gender identity differs from the sex they were assigned at birth), and nonbinary individuals (whose gender identity does not fit strictly within the categories of male or female). Recognizing and acknowledging male privilege is an essential first step toward dismantling the structures that perpetuate inequality (Kimmel, 2018).

One of the critical aspects of addressing male privilege is recognizing and normalizing gender diversity. In a society that often assumes gender based on appearances, names, or official documents like driver's licenses, trans and nonbinary individuals frequently face misgendering—being referred to by incorrect pronouns or gendered terms—which can lead to significant discrimination. Misgendering not only invalidates a person's identity but can also result in exclusion or unequal treatment in workplaces, healthcare, and social settings. To combat this, individuals can begin by sharing their pronouns when introducing themselves, helping to create a more inclusive environment for all genders. This small but impactful practice normalizes the idea that gender is not always apparent or binary. It signals respect for gender diversity and helps to challenge the gender assumptions that underlie much of male privilege (Serano, 2007).

Another key component of addressing male privilege is acknowledging the often unpaid and unrecognized labor that women, trans, and nonbinary people contribute to educating others about feminist and LGBTQ+ issues. This labor can place an unfair burden on marginalized groups, who are frequently expected to inform and enlighten those with gender or cisgender privilege. It's essential to recognize that both straight and queer cisgender men can benefit from this labor, though the dynamics of privilege may differ across sexual orientations.

On a day-to-day scale, cis men can address this imbalance by expressing genuine gratitude when receiving insights or resources from women and trans individuals, actively listening without expecting them to educate on demand, and showing commitment to learning independently about issues related to gender inequality and trans rights. Instead of relying on marginalized individuals to explain these issues, cis men might seek out books, articles, podcasts, and workshops on their own initiative. When possible, they could offer reciprocal support by sharing knowledge or resources in areas where they have expertise, fostering a more balanced exchange. Taking responsibility for one's own education, as bell hooks (2000) emphasizes, is an important way to show respect for the emotional and intellectual contributions of others and to work toward reducing reliance on marginalized individuals for these insights.

In professional and social spaces, men can actively work to be mindful of the space they occupy, especially when women and trans individuals are present. This awareness involves both physical space—such as avoiding dominating conversations or environments—and emotional space, noticing when men's voices or perspectives risk overshadowing those of marginalized genders. Cisgender men play an important role in educating other cis men about sexism and transphobia, speaking up whenever they witness discriminatory behavior or language. As Johnson (2014) notes, 'We are all implicated in systems of privilege and oppression, but this doesn't mean we are powerless; instead, we have a responsibility to interrupt these systems when we see them in action.' Silence in the face of harmful behavior only reinforces oppressive systems, making it essential for men to use their privilege to challenge and disrupt these narratives and practices.

Male privilege also influences the dynamics of personal relationships, particularly in heterosexual partnerships. Research shows that women often carry a disproportionate burden of emotional and physical labor within these relationships. Studies have found that women, even those who work full-time, are more likely to take on household chores and childcare responsibilities (Hochschild & Machung, 2012). Additionally, women are often expected to manage the emotional well-being of the relationship, a concept known as 'emotional labor,' which includes activities like resolving conflicts, remembering important dates, and providing emotional support (Erickson, 2005). This unequal distribution of labor reinforces traditional gender roles and places an ongoing strain on women, who may experience exhaustion and reduced personal well-being as a result. Men must become more aware of this imbalance and initiate discussions on how to make their relationships more equitable. Emotional maturity is a critical aspect of this work, as men are often socialized to rely on women for emotional support and labor. Developing emotional self-awareness and learning to manage one's own emotions without placing that burden on others is essential for fostering healthier, more balanced relationships (Gilligan, 1993).

In organizational settings, male privilege often manifests in the division of tasks that are traditionally considered "women's work," such as note-taking, organizing events, or handling administrative duties. Men can counteract this by being conscious of who is assigned or volunteers for these tasks and ensuring that these responsibilities are shared equitably. Volunteering for such roles helps to disrupt gendered expectations and creates a more balanced workplace environment (Williams & Dempsey, 2014). Additionally, using gender-inclusive language in professional and personal settings helps challenge the norms that reinforce male privilege. This includes avoiding gendered assumptions in language (e.g., referring to a group as "guys") and being respectful of people's chosen names and pronouns.

Finally, male privilege includes a certain level of detachment from laws and policies that primarily impact women, trans, and nonbinary individuals—particularly in areas of reproductive rights, sexual wellness, and pregnancy. Men often have the privilege of remaining unaffected by legislation that restricts access to abortion, birth control, and other reproductive healthcare, which are essential aspects of bodily autonomy. These laws disproportionately affect women and people assigned female at birth, leaving them with fewer choices and greater risks to their health, economic stability, and freedom. Men must actively engage with these issues, using their political voice and resources to support efforts that protect reproductive rights, oppose discriminatory legislation—such as restrictive bathroom bills targeting trans individuals—and advocate for workplace policies that ensure equality for all genders.

By speaking out and advocating on behalf of these rights, men help create a society that respects and values the autonomy of marginalized groups. When oppressive laws do pass, men should be proactive in finding ways to protect and support those most affected, such as by donating to abortion funds, supporting clinics that provide critical reproductive health services, or volunteering with organizations that defend LGBTQ+ rights. As Pascoe and Bridges (2016) suggest, understanding and challenging the systems that enforce gender inequality is essential for achieving a more just society. Through informed advocacy and action, men can help counterbalance the impact of restrictive laws and support the well-being of those who are most vulnerable to these policies.

Addressing male privilege requires ongoing self-reflection, education, and active participation in dismantling gender-based inequalities. It involves not only recognizing the advantages that come with being male but also using that privilege to challenge systems of oppression and to uplift those whose voices are often silenced or marginalized.

Actions Cisgender Men Can Take

1. State Your Pronouns
- Normalize stating your pronouns when introducing yourself to create an inclusive environment for trans and nonbinary people. This small act helps challenge assumptions about gender based on appearance or names.

2. Acknowledge and Compensate Emotional Labor
- Recognize the emotional labor women, trans, and nonbinary people often perform, especially when educating you or others on feminist and LGBTQ+ issues. Pay them for their time or acknowledge their efforts and seek to educate yourself.

3. Educate Other Cis Men
- Use your privilege to speak to other men about gender issues. Challenge sexism, misogyny, and transphobia when you encounter them in conversations, online, or in professional settings.

4. Be Mindful of the Space You Occupy
- Pay attention to the amount of physical, emotional, and conversational space you take up, especially in group settings where women and trans individuals are present. Avoid dominating discussions and make space for marginalized voices.

5. Speak Up Against Sexism and Transphobia
- Actively intervene when you witness sexist, misogynistic, or transphobic behavior. Silence reinforces oppressive behavior, so use your voice to challenge harmful narratives and actions.

6. Be Aware of Gendered Labor in Relationships

- In your relationships, notice the distribution of emotional, mental, and physical labor, especially with female or nonbinary partners. Have open conversations about how to make household chores, childcare, and emotional work more equitable.

7. Work on Emotional Maturity

- Develop emotional awareness and learn to process your feelings without relying on women or trans people to do the emotional labor for you. Seek therapy or other resources to work on emotional growth and encourage emotional openness with male friends.

8. Support Gender-Inclusive Policies

- Advocate for gender-inclusive policies in your workplace and community. Push for policies that support equitable parental leave, flexible work schedules, and accommodations for trans and nonbinary colleagues.

9. Use Gender-Inclusive Language

- Make a conscious effort to use gender-neutral terms when addressing groups or talking about people whose gender identities you don't know. For example, say "folks" or "everyone" instead of "guys" when referring to a group.

10. Be an Ally in Professional Settings

- In work environments, ensure that tasks traditionally relegated to women (like notetaking, organizing, or administrative work) are shared equitably. Volunteer for these tasks, rather than assuming women should do them.

11. Challenge Gender Stereotypes

- Actively work to dismantle harmful gender stereotypes, both in your own behavior and in conversations with others. Avoid reinforcing traditional masculine ideals like dominance, emotional suppression, or aggression.

12. Support Women and Trans Folks in Leadership
- Advocate for the promotion of women and trans individuals in leadership roles. Use your influence to support their career growth and speak up when you notice gender-based disparities in leadership and decision-making.

13. Pay Attention to Gender-Based Laws
- Stay informed about legislation affecting women, trans, and nonbinary individuals, such as reproductive rights, healthcare access, and employment protections. Use your voice and vote to support policies that protect these groups.

14. Mentor and Sponsor Marginalized Genders
- In professional or educational settings, consider mentoring or sponsoring women, trans, and nonbinary individuals. Use your privilege to help open doors and provide support that empowers marginalized people to advance their careers. When doing so, be mindful of potential pitfalls like mansplaining or overstepping boundaries. Offer guidance and resources without assuming you know more about their experiences or challenges; instead, listen actively and focus on understanding their goals and needs. By creating a respectful and collaborative relationship, you can provide support that truly uplifts and empowers them.

15. Engage in Self-Reflection
- Regularly reflect on your own actions, privileges, and biases. Seek feedback from women and trans people in

your life and be willing to change and improve your behavior based on what you learn.

I AM HETEROSEXUAL

Heterosexual privilege refers to the unearned societal advantages that heterosexual individuals experience over those who are queer or asexual. This privilege manifests in various forms, such as legal recognition of marriage and common-law partnerships, broader social acceptance, and the ability to navigate life without questioning or harassment because one's sexual orientation. Heterosexual privilege allows individuals to exist in the world without fear of discrimination, stereotyping, or needing to justify the legitimacy of their relationships. Often unnoticed by those who benefit from it, this privilege is pervasive, shaping how society views, treats, and marginalizes non-heterosexual individuals and their experiences (Yep, 2003).

A key aspect of dismantling heterosexual privilege is recognizing the diversity of sexual orientations and avoiding assumptions about others' sexuality. Society tends to assume heterosexuality as the default, leading to microaggressions that force queer people to either "come out" repeatedly or navigate spaces where they are presumed to be straight. By not assuming another person's sexuality and acknowledging that there are many valid ways to experience love and relationships, individuals can help create a more inclusive environment. This means recognizing queer relationships—whether married or not—as equally legitimate as heterosexual ones. These relationships should not be held to different standards of value or commitment based on their departure from heteronormativity (Ferguson, 2005).

Moreover, it is essential to actively protect and stand up for queer individuals in both social and legal contexts. This includes challenging stereotypes, interrupting homophobic jokes, and advocating for the rights of queer individuals. Passive acceptance is not enough; genuine allyship means using one's privilege to oppose harmful laws and policies that target queer people, such as those restricting marriage equality, adoption rights, or healthcare access. When LGBTQ+ individuals are not protected, they face increased risks of discrimination, isolation, and barriers to essential services—factors that can lead to mental health challenges, economic hardship, and reduced access to supportive communities. In the face of anti-LGBTQ+ legislation, heterosexual individuals have a responsibility to use their voices and resources to protect the rights and well-being of those who endure systemic oppression (Ghaziani, 2011).

Another key aspect of supporting queer individuals is respecting their coming-out journey. Coming out is a deeply personal process that varies from person to person, and it's crucial to let people come out on their own terms, in their own time. Pressuring someone to disclose their sexuality or inadvertently "outing" them can cause harm, jeopardize their safety, and undermine their agency. It is also important to provide ongoing support for queer individuals during and after this process, as coming out does not end with a single moment but is a continuous negotiation of identity in various social contexts (Rhoads, 1994).

Raising children in a way that normalizes queerness is another key step in challenging heterosexual privilege. By teaching children that queerness is just one of many ways to experience life and love, parents can help create a more inclusive and supportive world for future generations. This normalization is not just about accepting that others may be queer; it is about allowing children to explore and express their own potential queerness without fear or judgment. By ensuring that heterosexuality is not presented as the only "right" or "normal" way to live, parents can foster an environment where all forms of love and relationships are respected and valued.

Heterosexual privilege also influences how family members react when a loved one comes out. Family support plays a crucial role in shaping an individual's experience of their identity, and positive, affirming family environments significantly enhance the well-being of queer individuals. Offering unconditional support to queer family members, both during the coming-out process and afterward, is essential. When heterosexual family members actively challenge homophobic family norms, they help dismantle the privilege that marginalizes or excludes queer individuals from acceptance within their own families and society.

Finally, dismantling heterosexual privilege requires an openness to changing one's perspective. Just because heterosexual, monogamous, and long-lasting relationships may be ideal for some, it doesn't mean that they are right for everyone. Relationships that may look different from the traditional heteronormative model can still be healthy and fulfilling. Embracing diversity in relationship structures—

whether they be queer, non-monogamous, or otherwise—challenges the cultural dominance of heterosexuality and promotes greater equity and understanding in all aspects of life (Yep, 2003).

In summary, addressing heterosexual privilege involves recognizing and challenging the societal norms that marginalize queer individuals. By educating ourselves, raising inclusive children, supporting queer people through their coming-out journeys, and advocating for equal rights, we can contribute to a world where all sexual orientations are valued and respected. Only through this kind of active allyship can we begin to dismantle the structures of privilege that uphold heteronormativity and harm queer communities.

Actions Heteronormatives Can Take

1. Don't Assume Someone's Sexuality

- Avoid assuming that people are heterosexual based on appearances, names, or societal norms. Allow individuals to share their identity on their own terms.

2. Acknowledge Queer Relationships

- Treat queer relationships as equally valid and legitimate as heterosexual ones, regardless of whether they involve marriage. Avoid holding them to different standards of love or commitment.

3. Use Inclusive Language

- Incorporate gender-neutral and inclusive terms when talking about relationships. For example, use "partner" instead of "husband" or "wife" to avoid assuming someone's sexual orientation.

4. Stand Up Against Homophobia and Transphobia

- Actively intervene when you witness or hear homophobic, biphobic, or transphobic jokes, comments, or behavior. Remaining silent can be interpreted as approval, which subtly reinforces and normalizes discriminatory attitudes. By speaking up, you signal that such language and behavior are unacceptable, helping to create a more inclusive and respectful environment.

5. Support LGBTQ+ Rights Legislation

- Advocate for policies and laws that protect the rights of queer individuals. Support efforts that promote marriage equality, anti-discrimination protections, healthcare access, and more.

6. Respect the Coming-Out Process
- Allow queer individuals to come out on their own timeline and terms. Respect their privacy and journey and don't out them to others without their permission.

7. Normalize Queerness in Parenting
- Raise your children in an environment where being queer is normalized, so that they not only see it as normal in others, but also feel comfortable exploring their own identities, should they be queer.

8. Be Open to Diverse Relationship Models
- Recognize that not all people desire the same types of relationships. Just because you may value monogamous, heterosexual relationships doesn't mean they are the only healthy or valid way to live.

9. Support Queer Family Members
- Offer emotional support to family members who come out as queer. Be an advocate within your family, helping to create a loving and accepting environment for LGBTQ+ relatives.

10. Educate Yourself on LGBTQ+ Issues
- Take time to learn about the struggles, rights, and history of the LGBTQ+ community. Do not rely on queer individuals to educate you; take responsibility for your own learning.

11. Challenge Gender and Sexuality Norms
- Challenge the idea that heterosexuality is "normal" or "default." Recognize that all sexual orientations are equally valid and avoid reinforcing stereotypes or assumptions.

12. Be a Visible Ally

- Actively show your support for LGBTQ+ people, whether by attending Pride events, using your platform to amplify queer voices, or explicitly stating your stance on LGBTQ+ rights.

13. Create Inclusive Spaces

- In your workplace, social groups, or community, advocate for LGBTQ+-friendly environments. This includes gender-neutral bathrooms, inclusive policies—such as anti-discrimination protections, equitable benefits for same-sex partners, and diversity training—and respecting people's pronouns.

14. Diversify Your Media Consumption

- Watch films, read books, and follow media that represent LGBTQ+ people in a variety of ways. Expose yourself to diverse stories that go beyond stereotypes or tokenization.

15. Reevaluate Your Biases

- Regularly reflect on your own biases regarding gender and sexuality. Be open to changing your mind and evolving your understanding of what healthy, loving relationships can look like.

I AM WHITE

White privilege refers to the societal advantages that white individuals experience by virtue of their race. These advantages are often invisible to those who benefit from them but are woven into the fabric of social, political, and economic systems, affecting everything from daily interactions to long-term opportunities. White privilege operates in ways that normalize the experiences of white people as the standard, while marginalizing POC by limiting their access to the same opportunities and protections. Understanding white privilege is a critical step in dismantling the structures that perpetuate racial inequality and in building a more equitable society (McIntosh, 1989).

A key component of addressing white privilege is taking on the responsibility of educating friends, family members, and colleagues about racism and white privilege. It is not the responsibility of POC to explain these concepts to white people or to justify the impacts of racism on their lives. White individuals must do the work of learning about systemic racism, listening to the experiences of marginalized communities, and sharing that knowledge with those around them. This can help reduce the emotional burden placed on POC who are often expected to provide labor-intensive explanations of their lived experiences (DiAngelo, 2018). Furthermore, white individuals should be mindful of the spaces they occupy and the way they communicate, particularly when interacting with those whose first language may not be English. The expectation that others should adjust to white, English-speaking norms reinforces a power imbalance that stems from white privilege.

One of the most immediate actions white individuals can take to combat racism is to speak up when they witness it. If someone says something racist or acts offensively or dangerously toward a person of color, it is critical for bystanders to intervene. This can involve directly addressing the offender, calling out the behavior, or simply standing in solidarity with the person being targeted. Even if direct intervention isn't possible, showing support for the individual affected—through words or actions—can provide a sense of solidarity and safety. As researchers point out, white silence in the face of racism reinforces the systems of privilege and oppression that keep white supremacy intact (Tatum, 2017).

It is equally important to avoid microaggressions and harmful assumptions about people's nationality based solely on their race. Phrases like "Where are you really from?" imply that POC are inherently outsiders, regardless of their actual background. This question reinforces the idea that whiteness is the norm and that anyone who deviates from that standard doesn't truly belong, even if they were born and raised in the same country as the person asking. Teaching children about these harmful assumptions and encouraging them to embrace the full range of human diversity from an early age is essential for raising a generation that values inclusivity and challenges white privilege (Sue et al., 2007).

In addition to individual actions, systemic engagement is crucial. White individuals must pay attention to legislation and policies that affect communities of color, and actively work to support laws that promote equity and justice while opposing those that harm POC. Showing up for protests, events, and community organizations run by POC is another way to engage in the fight for racial justice. However, when participating in these spaces, it is important to avoid taking up too much space or assuming leadership roles in movements led by POC. White allies should center the voices and leadership of those directly affected by racial inequality and challenge other white people who dominate discussions or sideline POC during such events (Gassam, 2022).

An essential point in this work is to resist the temptation of "white saviorism." White saviorism occurs when white individuals position themselves as rescuers or protectors of POC, often out of a misguided sense of benevolence or superiority. This can manifest in actions where white people expect praise for their efforts or assume they know what marginalized communities need better than the people within those communities. As Cammarota (2011) discusses, white saviorism renders POC as incapable of helping themselves and strips them of their agency. Instead, true allyship requires trust that POC understand their own needs and can lead their own movements for change. White allies should be present to support and amplify those efforts, not to lead them or take credit.

Another form of meaningful allyship involves bearing witness to potential dangers faced by POC in interactions with law enforcement. In recent years, many high-profile cases of police violence against Black individuals have highlighted the disproportionate risk that POC face during encounters with the police. If a white person sees a POC being stopped by the police, one tangible action is to stay nearby and record the interaction if necessary. Simply being present and filming can act as a deterrent and may protect the individual from further harm (Alexander, 2012). This form of intervention is not about stepping in as a savior, but about using one's privilege to create a safer environment for those who are disproportionately targeted by law enforcement.

In conclusion, dismantling white privilege is a continuous process that requires white individuals to engage in self-reflection, education, and action. It involves speaking out against racism, supporting the leadership of POC in social justice movements, and recognizing the harmful effects of white saviorism. By taking these steps, white individuals can contribute to breaking down the systems of inequality that have privileged them for so long. The goal is not to feel guilt or defensiveness when confronted with one's own privilege, but to channel that awareness into meaningful action that supports racial justice.

Actions White People Can Take

1. Educate Yourself on White Privilege and Racism
- Take the initiative to read books, articles, and studies on white privilege, systemic racism, and anti-racism. Do not rely on POC to educate you on these topics; take responsibility for your own learning.

2. Speak Out Against Racism
- When you witness or hear racist comments, microaggressions, or behavior, speak up. Whether in social situations, the workplace, or online, challenge racist remarks and defend those affected.

3. Avoid Defensiveness When Confronted About Privilege
- If someone points out your white privilege or any unintended racism, take a moment to reflect. Avoid getting defensive or making it about your feelings. Use it as an opportunity to learn and grow.

4. Support Legislation That Promotes Racial Equity
- Stay informed about local, state, and national policies that affect POC, such as voting rights, police reform, and healthcare access. Use your voice and vote to support laws that dismantle systemic racism and promote equality.

5. Avoid Stereotyping or Microaggressions
- Refrain from asking harmful questions like "Where are you really from?" and avoid making assumptions about POC based on stereotypes. Acknowledge and respect the identity they share with you.

6. Diversify Your Media Consumption
- Make a conscious effort to watch films, read books, and follow media created by POC. This helps you understand

diverse perspectives and disrupts the dominance of white-centered narratives.

7. Teach Your Children About Racism and White Privilege

- Start conversations with your children about racism, white privilege, and equality from an early age. Encourage them to read books and watch media that center on the experiences of POC.

8. Use Your Platform to Amplify Voices of Color

- On social media or in your community, use your platform to share and amplify the voices and work of POC. Support their efforts, rather than centering yourself or seeking recognition for being an ally.

9. Support Businesses and Organizations Led by People of Color

- Make a conscious effort to support local businesses, nonprofits, and organizations run by POC. This contributes to economic equity and helps communities thrive.

10. Challenge White Saviorism

- Avoid the mindset that white people must "save" POC. Trust that POC know their own needs and can lead their own movements. Support their leadership without centering yourself or expecting praise.

11. Be a Witness in Potentially Dangerous Situations

- If you see a POC being harassed by the police or in a dangerous situation, stay present and film the interaction if necessary. Your presence can act as a deterrent and may prevent harm.

12. Engage in Conversations About Racism with Friends and Family

- Take responsibility for educating your friends and family about white privilege and systemic racism. Do not leave it to POC to always have to explain or justify their experiences.

13. Support Anti-Racism Protests and Movements

- Show up to protests, rallies, and events supporting racial justice, but be mindful not to take up too much space or leadership roles. Follow the lead of POC and ensure their voices are centered.

14. Hold Yourself Accountable

- Regularly reflect on your own biases and privilege. Recognize when you may have unintentionally reinforced white privilege or upheld systemic racism and take active steps to change.

15. Mentor and Sponsor People of Color

- In professional and community settings, mentor and sponsor individuals from underrepresented racial groups. Use your influence to help open doors for POC and provide meaningful support for their advancement.

I AM FINANCIALLY WEALTHY

Economic privilege refers to the unearned advantages and opportunities that individuals with wealth or financial stability experience over those without. These advantages allow people with economic privilege to navigate society with relative ease, accessing better education, healthcare, housing, and overall security. Economic privilege isn't just about having wealth—it's about the freedom from financial stress, the ability to make decisions without worrying about basic survival needs, and the power to shape one's environment and future. This privilege manifests in ways that often go unnoticed by those who benefit from it, but it has profound impacts on social equity and access to resources (Smith, 2014).

One expression of economic privilege is the freedom to give money without feeling the strain. For those with financial stability, donating money to those in need can be a powerful way to redistribute wealth and help close the economic gap. Rather than being afraid to spend money, those with economic privilege can make a significant impact by giving generously to causes that support the most vulnerable, such as giving directly to a houseless person, paying someone's medical bills, or covering a friend's rent. These actions help meet immediate needs and provide relief in an economic system that often fails those without wealth (Gittell & Wilder, 2016). Additionally, supporting grassroots organizations—particularly those run by or directly benefiting marginalized groups—ensures that money goes to the people who need it most. These organizations often work on the front lines of poverty and social injustice, making them vital for sustainable change.

However, being economically privileged also requires mindfulness about how wealth is spent and the environments one moves through. Those with economic privilege must be conscious of how they might inadvertently place financial burdens on others, such as by suggesting expensive restaurants or activities that friends may struggle to afford. Living a lifestyle that allows for more wealth redistribution rather than luxury consumption can be a way to consciously address the imbalances created by economic privilege (Kenworthy, 2007). Furthermore, staying connected to your community and understanding its needs is essential. By doing so, those with privilege can give strategically, ensuring their money and resources go where they are needed most, whether it's local mutual aid funds, community organizations, or grassroots movements that work directly with the people they aim to support.

Economic privilege fundamentally shapes how society views wealth and poverty, often favoring those who come from generational wealth. This privilege creates an inherent bias against those who lack access to resources over generations, making it more challenging for them to accumulate wealth. Reflecting on personal beliefs about money and the people who have it or lack it is essential for understanding this dynamic. Society often promotes assumptions that poor people are lazy or that wealthy people are inherently more deserving because they work harder. These beliefs perpetuate harmful stereotypes and overlook the systemic nature of poverty, including barriers to education, generational wealth disparities, and racial inequities (Rank, 2004). In reality, wealth is frequently accumulated through systemic advantages like inheritance, access to higher-quality education, and influential social networks, rather than individual effort alone. Recognizing this bias is key to a more equitable perspective—one that understands that wealth does not inherently signify moral worth or hard work, and that poverty is often a consequence of structural inequality rather than personal failings.

Gentrification is another way in which economic privilege is expressed and reinforced. When wealthier individuals move into lower-income neighborhoods, they often displace long-term residents, drive up housing costs, and contribute to the erasure of local cultures, particularly those of marginalized communities. Those with economic privilege should be mindful of their impact on the neighborhoods they move into, working to stand in solidarity with longtime residents rather than contributing to displacement. Gentrification disproportionately affects communities of color, who are often pushed out as neighborhoods become more appealing to wealthier, usually white, residents. Instead of calling the police on neighbors for minor issues, individuals can work to address the root causes of crime—often tied to poverty—by advocating for community resources and supporting initiatives that meet the basic needs of all residents (Zuk et al., 2018).

Shopping locally and supporting small businesses is another tangible way to redistribute wealth. Instead of funneling money into large corporations that often exploit workers, shopping at small, local businesses ensures that wealth circulates within the community. For business owners, economic privilege can be leveraged to offer affordable prices to local residents, while also ensuring that employees from the community are hired and paid a living wage that supports a high quality of life. You can also empower your employees by offering co-ownership opportunities or supporting their right to unionize, fostering a more equitable workplace where workers have a stake in the business and a stronger voice in decisions that affect their well-being. Supporting local economies is a key way to help communities build resilience against economic inequality (Schlosberg, 2019).

Finally, it's essential to teach the next generation to recognize their privilege and actively work against it. Instead of encouraging them to pursue wealth for its own sake—a path that can lead to prioritizing material gain over relationships, personal fulfillment, and community well-being—teach children to share resources and stand in solidarity with people from diverse economic backgrounds. Pursuing wealth as an end goal can foster detachment from community, increase social inequality, and perpetuate harmful cycles of consumerism. By teaching children to value all forms of work, regardless of pay, and to understand the systemic barriers that create wealth inequality, we instill a more equitable outlook. Encouraging them to stay connected to their communities and work toward social justice can plant the seeds for a future where economic privilege is more equitably shared (Piketty, 2014).

In summary, economic privilege permeates society in various forms, from the ability to give freely without financial strain to influencing how communities change and develop. Those with financial privilege have the power and responsibility to redistribute wealth, support local and marginalized communities, and challenge the societal structures that uphold inequality. Through conscious action, reflection on personal beliefs about wealth, and teaching the next generation, individuals can work to dismantle the systems that perpetuate economic privilege and build a more equitable society.

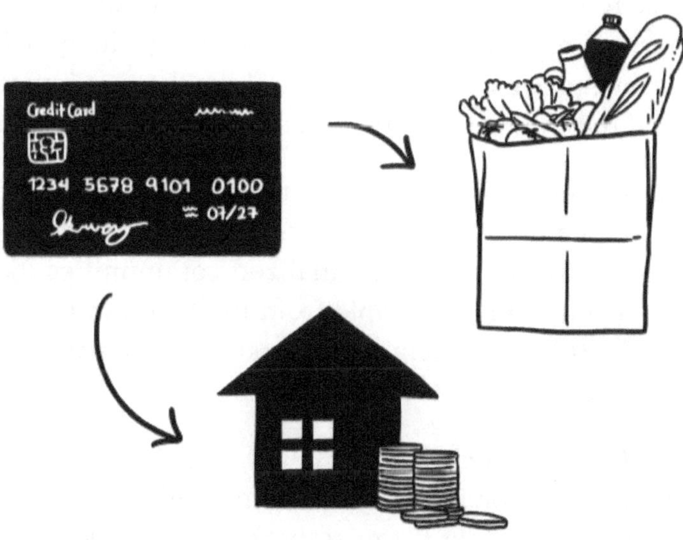

Actions Financially Wealthy Individuals Can Take

1. Redistribute Wealth
- Donate meaningful amounts to mutual aid funds, grassroots organizations, and individuals in need, considering your own position on the spectrum of financial privilege. Financial privilege exists on a sliding scale: someone with stable housing, employment, or savings may hold relative privilege compared to individuals experiencing houselessness or seeking assistance for basic needs, while still feeling less privileged than homeowners or those with substantial investments and retirement plans. Reflect on your own financial stability in relation to those around you, and if you're able, consider direct support through platforms like Venmo, CashApp, or GoFundMe to help cover essential expenses like rent, medical bills, or other urgent needs for people facing financial hardship. By recognizing where we hold privilege, we can contribute in ways that are impactful and relevant to our capacity and the needs of others.

2. Support Grassroots Organizations
- Research and donate to grassroots organizations that work directly with marginalized communities. Focus on groups run by people from those communities, as they are more likely to understand and address the community's needs effectively.

3. Live a Modest Lifestyle
- Reduce personal luxury spending and use the money saved to contribute to causes that help dismantle economic inequality. This also helps to avoid flaunting wealth in ways that further contribute to social disparities.

4. Be Mindful of Social Activities

- Be conscious of the financial situations of friends and colleagues when organizing social events. Avoid suggesting activities that require significant spending, like expensive dinners or trips, which can alienate people with less disposable income.

5. Participate in Local Communities

- Stay engaged in your community to understand the issues residents face. Support local projects and services that provide assistance and be informed about where your resources can make the most impact.

6. Challenge Your Assumptions About Wealth

- Reflect on personal beliefs about wealth, poverty, and merit. Challenge the idea that wealthy people are inherently more deserving or that poor people are lazy. Understand that systemic barriers prevent many from escaping poverty, and wealth is often accumulated through privilege.

7. Be Aware of Gentrification

- When moving into a new neighborhood, consider how your presence may affect local housing costs and displacement of long-term residents. Engage with your neighbors, advocate for rent control, and support efforts that protect marginalized communities from being pushed out.

8. Support Local and Small Businesses

- Shop from and invest in local, small businesses rather than large corporations. This keeps wealth circulating within the community and supports businesses that are more likely to provide fair wages and opportunities.

9. Hire Locally

- If you own a business, hire employees from the local community, particularly from economically disadvantaged groups. Offer fair wages and benefits, ensuring that your business contributes positively to the local economy.

10. Fund Social and Environmental Justice Initiatives

- Use your wealth to support initiatives that address social, racial, and environmental justice. Prioritize projects that aim to dismantle systemic inequality and provide sustainable, long-term solutions for marginalized groups.

11. Advocate for Progressive Taxation

- Support policies that advocate for higher taxes on the wealthy and corporations. These funds can be used to improve public services, reduce poverty, and increase access to resources like healthcare and education.

12. Invest in Affordable Housing

- Donate to or invest in projects that provide affordable housing for low-income families. Support organizations fighting for housing rights and policies that prevent the displacement of vulnerable populations.

13. Teach Children About Economic Privilege

- Educate your children about wealth inequality and privilege. Encourage them to share resources, stay connected with people from different socioeconomic backgrounds, and avoid the pursuit of wealth for its own sake.

14. Listen to and Amplify Marginalized Voices

- Elevate the voices of those who are directly affected by poverty and economic inequality. Support their leadership in social justice movements and ensure that your wealth and influence are used to amplify their causes rather than centering yourself.

15. Make Ethical Investments

- Align your investments with your values. Divest from industries that exploit workers, harm the environment, or perpetuate inequality, and invest in companies that prioritize sustainability, fair wages, and social responsibility.

I AM THIN

Thin privilege refers to the unearned societal advantages that people with thinner bodies experience over individuals with larger bodies. These advantages manifest in various aspects of life, from social interactions and healthcare to professional environments and public spaces. Thin privilege operates within a culture that prizes and idealizes slim bodies while stigmatizing and marginalizing those who don't conform to these societal beauty standards. Importantly, the term "fat" is not inherently improper or negative; it can be a neutral descriptor for body size. However, in a society shaped by thin privilege, individuals with fat bodies often face discrimination, shame, and reduced access to basic rights and opportunities—consequences that may be invisible to those who benefit from thin privilege (Bacon & Aphramor, 2011).

One common way thin privilege expresses itself is through the design of communal spaces. Public and private spaces, such as classrooms, theaters, offices, and restaurants, are often designed with smaller body sizes in mind. This can make it difficult or uncomfortable for individuals with larger bodies—those whose size or proportions differ from standard seating or spacing—to navigate or use these spaces. For example, seating in theaters or airplanes is often too narrow, leading to embarrassment and discomfort for people who need more room. People with thin privilege may not realize this daily struggle, as their bodies naturally fit into these environments. Being mindful of space inclusivity, such as ensuring communal areas have enough room for people of all sizes to move comfortably, is one way to help dismantle thin privilege and make spaces more accessible for everyone (Farrell, 2011).

Healthcare is another area where thin privilege is deeply ingrained, even though weight and health can sometimes intersect. While certain weight-related health risks may exist, it is essential to recognize that body size alone is not an absolute indicator of health. Individuals with larger bodies often face biased treatment from medical professionals, who may quickly dismiss their symptoms as solely weight-related, even when the underlying causes are unrelated. This bias can lead to delayed diagnoses and inadequate care, preventing patients from receiving the timely and comprehensive treatment they need. The assumption that larger bodies are inherently unhealthy can result in individuals being unfairly blamed for their own health issues, regardless of their actual habits or conditions.

Healthcare professionals have a responsibility to approach each patient with compassion and avoid making assumptions based on body size alone. Thin individuals are not automatically healthy, just as larger individuals are not automatically unhealthy. Distinguishing between health and cultural ideals around body size allows for more unbiased, patient-centered care. Every patient, regardless of size, deserves attentive, respectful, and comprehensive medical care (Tomiyama et al., 2018).

The way society views people of different sizes is deeply influenced by long-standing stereotypes. Fat folks are often associated with laziness, lack of discipline, and poor health, while thin folks are seen as symbols of success, intelligence, and desirability. These biases shape the way people interact with individuals of different sizes and reinforce weight stigma. Contrary to the belief that shaming people for their weight can motivate them to lose weight, research shows that weight stigma often leads to negative outcomes, including lower self-esteem, disordered eating, and avoidance of healthcare (Bacon, 2010). Acknowledging and challenging these biases within ourselves and others is crucial in dismantling thin privilege and the societal harms associated with fatphobia.

While many people experience harm from anti-fatness, it is essential to recognize that some individuals face genuine life-threatening risks due to fatphobia. This is especially true for POC and those living in poverty, who may experience intersecting forms of discrimination. People with larger bodies are often discriminated against in employment, housing, and even education, limiting their opportunities and impacting their quality of life. For some, the stigma and bias associated with their size can lead to social isolation and mental health struggles. Society's focus on thinness as the ideal standard not only marginalizes people with larger bodies but actively endangers their well-being (Saguy, 2013).

One way to start addressing thin privilege is to engage with people in your life who are larger than you. Having open, respectful conversations about their experiences with weight stigma, the language they prefer when discussing body size, and how you can support them is a crucial step. These conversations should center the needs and experiences of the person you're supporting, rather than focusing on your own feelings or insecurities about your body. It's important to listen without making assumptions and to avoid projecting your own body image concerns onto the discussion. It's important to listen without making assumptions and to avoid projecting your own body image concerns onto the conversation. By creating a supportive and inclusive environment, you can help reduce the harm caused by weight stigma and provide meaningful support to those affected by anti-fat bias (Cooper, 2016).

It's also essential to be mindful of how we talk to and treat children. Weight stigma can have long-lasting effects on a child's mental and physical health, leading to issues such as eating disorders, depression, and avoidance of medical care. Instead of focusing on a child's weight, it is more beneficial to provide them with access to healthy, nourishing foods and encourage a positive relationship with their bodies. Children need environments that support their emotional and physical well-being, where they can grow up without being taught that their worth is tied to their size (Puhl et al., 2013). Teaching children to embrace diversity in body sizes from a young age helps foster a healthier self-image and promotes empathy for others.

In conclusion, thin privilege operates in many areas of life, from the design of public spaces to healthcare to societal attitudes toward weight. It reinforces harmful stereotypes and marginalizes individuals with larger bodies, limiting their access to resources, opportunities, and dignity. To dismantle thin privilege, individuals must be mindful of how they talk about bodies, create inclusive environments, and challenge their biases. Engaging in respectful conversations with people of larger bodies and promoting body diversity in all spaces—especially for children—can help break down the damaging effects of weight stigma. By working to dismantle thin privilege, society can move toward a more inclusive and equitable future for people of all body sizes.

Actions Thin Folks Can Take

1. Acknowledge Thin Privilege
- Recognize that thin privilege exists and that, as a thinner person, you may experience unearned advantages in areas like healthcare, job opportunities, social acceptance, and accessibility in public spaces.

2. Make Communal Spaces Accessible
- Ensure that spaces you control or design—such as offices, classrooms, restaurants, and theaters—have seating and pathways that accommodate people of all sizes. Advocate for more spacious seating in public and communal areas.

3. Refrain from Commenting on Others' Bodies
- Avoid making comments about other people's weight, even if intended as a compliment. Focus on attributes that don't center on size, as constant attention to body size can be harmful and reinforce societal obsession with thinness.

4. Reject Fat phobic Health Advice
- Don't offer unsolicited health or weight-loss advice to people with larger bodies. Recognize that body size is not an indicator of health and that it's inappropriate to assume someone's health based on their appearance.

5. Advocate for Size-Inclusive Healthcare
- Encourage healthcare professionals to treat patients of all sizes with dignity and respect. Speak out against fatphobia in medical settings, where larger individuals often face biased or inadequate care.

6. Examine Your Biases About Body Size
- Reflect on how you think about body size. Do you

equate thinness with health, beauty, or intelligence? Do you assume that people with larger bodies are lazy or unhealthy? Challenge these stereotypes and work to unlearn harmful biases.

7. Support Anti-Discrimination Policies

- Advocate for policies in workplaces, schools, and healthcare settings that prevent weight-based discrimination. Push for laws that protect people from size discrimination in hiring, housing, and public accommodations.

8. Create Body-Positive Environments for Children

- Avoid discussing weight, dieting, or body size with children. Instead, focus on healthy habits, positive body image, and self-care. Create spaces where children can feel comfortable and accepted regardless of their size.

9. Support Media That Challenges Thin Ideals

- Watch and promote media that represent body diversity and avoid content that glorifies thinness as the ideal. Support creators, influencers, and movements that promote body acceptance for all sizes.

10. Challenge Fatphobic Jokes and Remarks

- Speak up when you hear Fatphobic comments, jokes, or micro aggressions. Even casual remarks can reinforce harmful stereotypes, so you should intervene to create a more inclusive environment.

11. Listen to Fat People

- Have open conversations with friends, family members, or colleagues who are larger than you. Ask how you can be more supportive and learn about their experiences with weight stigma, but make sure to center their needs rather than your own feelings.

12. Shop at and Support Size-Inclusive Brands

- Support clothing and product brands that offer a wide range of sizes and cater to diverse body types. Avoid companies that exclude larger bodies from their sizing range or marketing campaigns.

13. Avoid Participating in Diet Culture

- Challenge societal norms that promote dieting and weight loss as inherently good. Avoid discussing diets, weight loss goals, or "clean eating" in social situations, as these conversations can perpetuate the belief that thinner is better.

14. Advocate for Size-Inclusive Workplace Practices

- Encourage your employer to ensure that chairs, uniforms, and other workspaces are comfortable for employees of all sizes. Support policies that prevent weight discrimination in the hiring process and promote diversity in body types at work.

15. Recognize the Intersection of Fatphobia and Other Forms of Oppression

- Understand that fatphobia often intersects with other forms of discrimination, such as racism, ableism, and classism. Recognize the compounded harm that individuals at these intersections face, and advocate for inclusive, intersectional approaches to addressing body stigma.

REFERENCES & FURTHER READINGS

Alexander, M. (2020). *The new Jim Crow: Mass incarceration in the age of colorblindness* (10th ed.). The New Press.

Andersen, K., & Kuhn, K. (Directors). (2014). *Cowspiracy: The sustainability secret* [Film]. A.U.M. Films.

Ariès, P. (1962). *Centuries of childhood: A social history of family life.* Vintage Books.

Arora, R. (2020, July 11). *The fallacy of white privilege—And how it's corroding society.* New York Post. https://nypost.com/2020/07/11/the-fallacy-of-white-privilege-and-how-its-corroding-society/

Bacon, L. (2010). *Health at every size: The surprising truth about your weight.* BenBella Books.

Bacon, L., & Aphramor, L. (2011). Weight science: Evaluating the evidence for a paradigm shift. *Nutrition Journal, 10*(1). https://doi.org/10.1186/1475-2891-10-9

Black, L. L., & Stone, D. (2005). Expanding the definition of privilege: The concept of social privilege. *Journal of Multicultural Counseling and Development, 33*(4), 243–255. https://doi.org/10.1002/j.2161-1912.2005.tb00020.x

Brown, B. (2012). *Daring greatly: How the courage to be vulnerable transforms the way we live, love, parent, and lead.* Gotham Books.

Brueck, J. F. (2017). *Veganism in an oppressive world: A vegans-of-color community project.* Sanctuary Publishers.

Burgard, D. (2009). What is "health at every size"? In E. Rothblum & S. Solovay (Eds.), *The fat studies reader* (pp. 42–53). New York University Press.

Cammarota, J. (2011). Blindsided by the avatar: White saviors and allies out of Hollywood and in education. *Review of Education, Pedagogy, and Cultural Studies, 33*(3), 242–259. https://doi.org/10.1080/10714413.2011.585287

Cooper, C. (2016). *Fat activism: A radical social movement.* HammerOn Press.

Crenshaw, K. (2015, September 24). Why intersectionality can't wait. *The Washington Post.* https://www. washingtonpost.com/news/in-theory/wp/2015/09/24/ why-intersectionality-cant-wait/

Crist, E. (2012). Abundant earth and human population: A problem of contradictions. *Population and Environment, 34*(1), 31–48. https://doi.org/10.1007/s11111-011-0153-2

Crosley-Corcoran, G. (2014, May 8). *Explaining white privilege to A broke white person.* HuffPost. https://www.huffpost. com/entry/explaining-white-privilege-to-a-broke-white-person_b_5269255

Croteau, J. M., Talbot, D. M., Lance, T. S., & Evans, N. J. (2002). A qualitative study of the interplay between privilege and oppression. *Journal of Multicultural Counseling and Development, 30*(4), 239–258. https://doi.org/10.1002/j.2161-1912.2002.tb00522.x

DiAngelo, R. (2018). *White fragility: Why it's so hard for white people to talk about racism.* Beacon Press.

Du Bois, W. E. B. (1903). *The souls of Black folk: Essays and sketches* (2nd ed.). A. C. McClurg & Co.

Dunn, D. S. (2019). *Understanding the experience of disability: Perspectives from social and rehabilitation psychology.* Oxford University Press.

Erickson, R. J. (2005). Why emotion work matters: Sex, gender, and the division of household labor. *Journal of Marriage and Family, 67*(2), 337–351. https://doi.org/10.1111/j.0022-2445.2005.00120.x

Farrell, A. E. (2011). *Fat shame: Stigma and the fat body in American culture.* NYU Press.

Ferguson, R. A. (2005). *Aberrations in Black: Toward a queer of color critique.* University of Minnesota Press.

Fredrickson, B. L. (2001). The role of positive emotions in positive psychology: The broaden-and-build theory of positive emotions. *American Psychologist, 56*(3), 218–226. https://doi.org/10.1037/0003-066X.56.3.218

Friedman, C., & Owen, A. L. (2017). Defining disability: Understandings of and attitudes toward ableism and disability identity. *Disability Studies Quarterly, 37*(1).

Gassam, J. (2022). What is white saviorism and how does it show up in your workplace? *Forbes.* https://www.forbes.com/sites/janicegassam/2022/09/30/what-is-white-saviorism-and-how-does-it-show-up-in-your-workplace/?sh=57d9ff20126d

Ghaziani, A. (2011). *The dividends of dissent: How conflict and culture work in lesbian and gay marches on Washington.* University of Chicago Press.

Gilligan, C. (1993). *In a different voice: Psychological theory and women's development.* Harvard University Press.

Girshick, L. B. (2014). In the doing and the being. In W. Tuttle (Ed.), *Circles of compassion: Connecting issues of justice* (pp. 54–62). Vegan Publishers.

Gittell, R., & Wilder, M. (2016). *Empowerment zones and urban economic development: Social capital, political capital, and economic development.* SAGE Publications.

Goodfellow, A. (2022). *Innocence and corruption.* Freedom Press.

Goodley, D. (2014). *Dis/ability studies: Theorising disablism and ableism.* Routledge.

Gordon, A. [@yrfatfriend]. (n.d.). *Posts* [Instagram profile]. Instagram. Retrieved November 13, 2020, from https://www.instagram.com/yrfatfriend

Hochschild, A. R., & Machung, A. (2012). *The second shift: Working families and the revolution at home.* Penguin Books.

hooks, b. (2000). *All about love: New visions.* Harper Collins.

hooks, b. (2000). *Feminism is for everybody: Passionate politics.* South End Press.

https://doi.org/10.18061/dsq.v37i1.5061

Johnson, A. G. (2014). *The gender knot: Unraveling our patriarchal legacy.* Temple University Press

Jones, P. (2014). *The oxen at the intersection.* Lantern Books.

Joshi, K. Y. (2006). *New roots in America's sacred ground: Religion, race, and ethnicity in Indian America*. Rutgers University Press.

Joshi, K. Y. (2020). *White Christian privilege: The illusion of religious equality in America*. New York University Press.

Joy, M. (2019). *Powerarchy: Understanding the psychology of oppression for social transformation*. Berrett-Koehler Publishers.

Kauffman, C. M., & Martin, P. L. (2017). Can rights of nature make development more sustainable? Why some Ecuadorian lawsuits succeed and others fail. *World Development, 92*(3), 130–142. https://doi.org/10.1016/j.worlddev.2016.11.017

Kenworthy, L. (2007). Inequality and growth: Recent evidence. *American Behavioral Scientist, 50*(5), 584–602. https://doi.org/10.1177/0002764206295008

Kimmel, M. (2018). *Angry white men: American masculinity at the end of an era*. Nation Books.

Kimmel, M. S. (2018). *Privilege: A reader*. Routledge.

Kohn, A. (2005). *Unconditional parenting: Moving from rewards and punishments to love and reason*. Atria Books.

Latner, J. D., & Stunkard, A. J. (2003). Getting worse: The stigmatization of obese children. *Obesity Research, 11*(3), 452–456. https://doi.org/10.1038/oby.2003.61

Lazarus, A. (2014, February 12). *20 ways to not be a gentrifier*. The Guardian. https://www.theguardian.com/cities/2014/feb/12/oakland-20-ways-not-be-gentrifier

Mah, A. (2014, February 12). Oakland: 20 ways not to be a gentrifier. *The Guardian*. https://www.theguardian.com/cities/2014/feb/12/oakland-20-ways-not-be-gentrifier

Malik, K. (2020, June 14). "White privilege" is a distraction, leaving racism and power untouched. *The Guardian.* https://www.theguardian.com/commentisfree/2020/jun/14/white-privilege-is-a-lazy-distraction-leaving-racism-and-power-untouched

Maslow, A. H. (1943). A theory of human motivation. *Psychological Review, 50*(4), 370–396. https://doi.org/10.1037/h0054346

McIntosh, P. (1989, July). White privilege: Unpacking the invisible knapsack. *Peace and Freedom Magazine,* 10–12. https://med.umn.edu/sites/med.umn.edu/files/2022-12/White-Privilege_McIntosh-1989.pdf

McIntosh, P. (2019). *On privilege, fraudulence, and teaching as learning.* Routledge.

Michigan Coalition to End Domestic and Sexual Violence. (2020, September 9). *The harmful impact of my neurotypical privilege at work.* https://mcedsv.org/2020/09/the-harmful-impact-of-my-neurotypical-privilege-at-work/

Mingus, M. (2011). *Changing the framework: Disability justice.* Leaving Evidence Blog.

Monson, C. (Director). (2018). *Dominion* [Film]. Aussie Farms.

Neff, K. D. (2003). Self-compassion: An alternative conceptualization of a healthy attitude toward oneself. *Self and Identity, 2*(2), 85–101. https://doi.org/10.1080/15298860309032

Nibert, D. (2002). *Animal rights/human rights: Entanglements of oppression and liberation.* Rowman & Littlefield.

Nibert, D. (2013). *Animal oppression and human violence: Domesecration, capitalism, and global conflict.* Columbia University Press.

Oluo, I. (2018). *So you want to talk about race.* Seal Press.

Pascoe, C. J., & Bridges, T. (2016). *Exploring masculinities: Identity, inequality, continuity and change.* Oxford University Press.

Pellow, D. (2014). *Total liberation: The power and promise of animal rights and the radical earth movement.* University of Minnesota Press.

Petriglieri, G., Ashford, S. J., & Wrzesniewski, A. (2019). Agility in the workplace: Navigating the global shifts in talent and careers. *Academy of Management Annals, 13*(1), 1–55.

Piketty, T. (2014). *Capital in the twenty-first century.* Harvard University Press.

Puhl, R. M., & Brownell, K. D. (2001). Bias, discrimination, and obesity. *Obesity Research, 9*(12), 788–805. https://doi.org/10.1038/oby.2001.108

Puhl, R. M., Latner, J. D., O'Brien, K., Luedicke, J., Forhan, M., & Danielsdottir, S. (2013). Cross-national perspectives about weight-based bullying in youth: Nature, extent and remedies. *Pediatric Obesity, 8*(5), 420–428. https://doi.org/10.1111/ijpo.12051

Rank, M. R. (2004). *One nation, underprivileged: Why American poverty affects us all.* Oxford University Press.

Rhoads, R. A. (1994). Coming out in college: The struggle for a queer identity. *Journal of College Student Development, 35*(3), 177–186. https://doi.org/10.5860/choice.32-4800

Rothblum, E., & Solovay, S. (Eds.). (2009). *The fat studies reader.* NYU Press.

Saguy, A. C. (2013). *What's wrong with fat?* Oxford University Press.

Schlosberg, D. (2019). *Defining environmental justice: Theories, movements, and nature.* Oxford University Press.

Sebastian, C. (2020, July 6). *Joe Biden, veganism, and the unbearable privilege of talking about privilege.* Christopher Sebastia. https://www.christophersebastian.info/post/joe-biden-veganism-and-the-unbearable-privilege-of-talking-about-privilege

Serano, J. (2007). *Whipping girl: A transsexual woman on sexism and the scapegoating of femininity.* Seal Press.

Singer, P. (1975). *Animal liberation: A new ethics for our treatment of animals.* HarperCollins.

Singh, A. A. (2019). *The racial healing handbook: Practical activities to help you challenge privilege, confront systemic racism, and engage in collective healing.* New Harbinger Publications.

Smith, M. (2014). *The cost of privilege: Taking on the system of white supremacy and racism.* NYU Press.

Sue, D. W., Capodilupo, C. M., Torino, G. C., Bucceri, J. M., Holder, A. M. B., Nadal, K. L., & Esquilin, M. (2007). Racial microaggressions in everyday life: Implications for clinical practice. *American Psychologist, 62*(4), 271–286. https://doi.org/10.1037/0003-066X.62.4.271

Tatum, B. D. (2017). *Why are all the Black kids sitting together in the cafeteria? And other conversations about race.* Basic Books.

Taylor, S. (2017). *Beasts of burden: Animal and disability liberation.* The New Press

Tomiyama, A. J., Carr, D., Granberg, E. M., Major, B., Robinson, E., Sutin, A. R., & Brewis, A. (2018). How and why weight stigma drives the obesity 'epidemic' and harms health. *BMC Medicine, 16*(1). https://doi.org/10.1186/s12916-018-1116-5

White, L. (1967). The historical roots of our ecological crisis. *Science, 155*(3767), 1203–1207. https://doi.org/10.1126/science.155.3767.1203

Williams, J. C., & Dempsey, R. (2014). *What works for women at work: Four patterns working women need to know.* NYU Press.

Wong, A. (2020). *Disability visibility: First-person stories from the twenty-first century.* Vintage.

Yep, G. A. (2003). The violence of heteronormativity in communication studies. *Journal of Homosexuality, 45*(2-4), 11–59. https://doi.org/10.1300/j082v45n02_02

Zelizer, V. A. (1985). *Pricing the priceless child: The changing social value of children.* Princeton University Press.

Zuk, M., Bierbaum, A. H., Chapple, K., Gorska, K., & Loukaitou-Sideris, A. (2018). Gentrification, displacement, and the role of public investment. *Journal of Planning Literature, 33*(1), 31–44. https://doi.org/10.1177/0885412217716439